Note to the Reader

From My Eye to the Sky contains the following: racism, child neglect, strong language, sexual content, suicide, ableism, religious themes, political themes, and gore.

Dedicated to my comrades

From My Eye To The Sky

J.V. Sadler

J.V. Sadler

Copyright © 2024 by J.V. Sadler

All rights reserved.

No portion of this book may be reproduced in any form without written permission from the publisher or author, except as permitted by U.S. copyright law.

Library of Congress Control Number: 2024906292

Hardback ISBN: 979-8-9896242-3-2

Previously Published Poems

"The Sea Tamer" was first published in *Hope Springs Eternal: An Anthology of Hopeful Poetry* (2023) by Simple Simons Press

"Unshackle the River" was first published in *Songs for Wild Ohio* (2023) by Last Exit Press

"A Poem for Charles" was first published in *Voices of the Real 8* (2024) by Poetry Is Life Publishing

"Palestine on my mind" was first published in *For A Better World* (2024) by SOS ART

Contents

Introduction	1
From My Eye to the Sky	3
Hope is	5
Life is	6
Wild Onion	7
Such terrible-sounding love	8
pappy said this would happen one day	9
Unpoetic	11
A Frustrated Poem	12
Lynch'n	13
Icarus XX	15
A Bright Sunny Day	18
Alien Pussy	19
Satisfied, so satisfying	21
Devil's Speak	23
in the mirror	26

[Here I Am]	27
Willful Whispers	32
No more hopeful shit	33
The Wanderer	34
Your Language	35
Resilience is not my forte	37
The Sea Tamer	39
Unshackle the River	41
The Water of Fun	43
Haiku for you	45
When the Doc told me I was bipolar II	46
Crazy Love	48
Show Me God	49
A Poem for Charles	50
Ain't Chu Tired?	54
Palestine on my mind	56
White Guilt	57
Shake hands with a President	58
Pork Roast	59
Blue Lives	60
Da Birdz	61

Mutt Dog	64
'Tis Black or White	67
On Violence	70
Molotov Cocktails	72
Remembering Fred	73
Not So Fairy Tale	75
New Jersey Turnpike	77
Say "Thank you"	80
Saturday Morning Cartoons	81
Ode to the Colored Trumpet Boy	82
Just when I thought I could write about men	84
Don't look at me like that	86
Dear tree that the white people cut down	88
The Cookout	89
Solidarity Party	90
The Cookout Part Two	91
Bee Booty	93
Rejoice	95
Got my eye on it	97

Introduction

I DECLARE THAT I AM A POWERFUL WOMAN. This is the first time that I've ever recognized my divinity. *From My Eye to the Sky* is an homage to my mind, to the people out here doing the good work, and to liberation—liberation from capitalism, from white supremacy, and from all the "-isms" and "-phobias" that exist in this world. But liberation *from* something must mean a liberation *to* something.

Sankofa is, a word in Twi that means "go back and get it." The Akan Sankofa bird reaches its long neck behind itself to reach an egg. Sankofa means to look toward the ancestors and retrieve the lessons they taught us, leaving behind their mistakes, and always improving our ways of living. My liberation gazes toward the sky, toward a free Africa, and unfettered, radical love.

Daring to be vulnerable, while writing, I placed a slice of myself into each poem. This is by far my most vulnerable work yet. So, I thank you for taking this journey with me. I hope that those who read *From My Eye to the Sky* are inspired to create, build community, and keep fighting the good fight.

From My Eye to the Sky

We shall be free

. . . one day

We will walk on water

. . . one day

We can sing our mothers' songs

as she prepares collard for supper

Maybe lay on her lap and tell

her all our troubles

I'll tell stories to my grandbabies [If I ever have children]

of a liberated Africa

and sip on mango nectar

Ichor from a cardboard carton

Dreams of Mutulu, Assata, Malcolm, and Huey

Dreams of finally livin'—I mean *real* livin'

Finally seeing what all this hoopla these birds call flyin'

is all about

Hope is

Hope is a rickety train

riding on the tracks of faith through the tunnel of doubt

It is a wild locomotive carrying such explosive cargo—

possibility

Toot the horn of opportunity,

avoiding the avalanches of disappointment

It winds and bends through the land of darkness

with a lone lantern hung on its front

Life is

like walking through a thunderstorm

Blindfolded and barefooted

It is as feet's pain

on cracked concrete, like the winces and whines

from a sharp pang

like finally reaching your destination

with bandaged legs.

Wild Onion

Oh, wild thing

Grow so tall, so slender

abreast white irises

—A green alien among

virgin white maidens—

Taint my garden with your pungent

scents

No, you will not be made useful

in a stew or as garnish to plate

Instead, rest here

next to rotten fish

excrement

Forgotten Furniture

Such terrible-sounding love

It smells like rain nearing to come

tastes of ammonia

and feels as the hard shell of a tortoise

No, it is certainly not what I expected

Me wanting gardenia scent; perfume

Perhaps strawberries and mangoes,

the feeling of a white feather boa against my shoulders

Instead, I must settle for bleach

basic liquids dissolving skin

Knock against wood—

a hard thing that I'll never penetrate

pappy said this would happen one day

That I would fall in love with a

no-good sucker like you

That I would wonder if I was worth love

because of you

That I would give my all

to you

That I would find my own body

foreign and alien

after you've touched it

How small I . . .

How scared I . . .

How silent I . . .

Be

But enough of that

I think it's time

I finally let you go

Unpoetic

I wish I had something more poetic to say,

but I don't

All I want to do is

vomit

all my rage

onto the lined paper

and cry me

a good cry

A Frustrated Poem

Everyone's smiling

Everyone's smiling

But we all dying

DEAD

Lynch'n

Cry hymn

Thy wry crypt

dry cyst

Why, hwyl

pry myrrh

Gyp nymphs &

myth glyphs &

Try, try spry

So fly

Fly by

Fly by

Shhh

By-By

Icarus XX

three . . .

                Rumbling and shaking

two . . .

                Nausea and vertigo

one . . .

                    To the star

His hands are sweaty, trembling.

He glances at the panel, whose colors become a blur.

           Static

"Copy that."

Static

His laughter bounces

from the metal interior back into his face.

Sounds and beeps — not the good kind

His hands are red

Cherry tomatoes

His face is ruby

Dorothy's slippers

This means he's getting closer.

The rattling and banging continues.

The yellow colors turn into fiery violets.

Icarus XX

They let him name it; It was his baby

Static

"Roger"

He flicks switches in a manner unintelligible to the uneducated eye. His feet are burning now.

But he is almost there

                    To the star

A Bright Sunny Day

Eyes seeping turning bleeding crying tearing calling crippling jumping seeing fleeing falling fighting

    Eyes burning churning chipping dusting rusting lying frying trying hailing sailing flailing trailing wailing

        the light is too hot but they stare at the light is too hot but they stare at the light is too hot

How long can they look until their brains go

POP!

Alien Pussy

They say alien pussy tastes like citrus
when it cries, they laugh

How are they supposed to speak its language
it could be liking it, for all that they know

Universities, Agencies, Governments
they're all there

This is for scientific investigation
a necessary evil, they say

They have a foxy mama, Black and Bold
she dances

The thing copies her moves
under bright industrial lights

Her face is downturned
they are paying her extra

And they are getting bonuses
I hope the six figures are worth it

They say alien pussy tastes like citrus

the cameras record

The red dot captures everything they do
some dude

They pay him to upload it
it is wailing louder now

Five thousand views within minutes
its appendages are held

Pictures snap, and lenses shutter
this is for scientific investigation

A necessary evil, they say
twenty million views

The thing is shoved
into its cage

And it waits, alone
to be told what to do

They say alien pussy tastes like citrus
And that it doesn't feel a thing

Satisfied, so satisfying

when the embrace of a friend is warm and gay,

when the kisses are electrifying

and the night purple as grape medicine,

when the cookies in the oven

are gooey and chunky, when

the crackle crackles just right,

when the lines are straight and

the curves are oh so curvy,

when the zipper zips all the way

and the flapper flaps on stage,

when the secret is kept

and when it is finally told, when

the ice is cold, and

the fire hot on the stove, when

the murderer claims his favorite victim

and the pervert fondles a nice bottom,

and the devil can watch the world burn.

Devil's Speak

I command the devil,

Come, sit down and talk to me

Look at my skin, Black skin!

they say everybody's made in God's image

Not me

—coal-kissed, rub and rub and rub

the soot off till my brown is pink and raw—

I was made in darkness

like the moment before God's seven days

like the moment before the atoms clashed together:

Big Bang

Little white kids be scared of the dark

They say you're the monster lurkin' in suburban closets

but what's scarier to a WASP than a little Black boy

selling bottled water on the corner?

Satan, they call us demons

Are my ancestors down there with you?

The Africans who ain't know Jesus' name

The Africans from Yorubaland who sang with orisha instead of angels

The Black Women called succubus after being raped

How they doin'?

They doin' alright

How they doin'?

They doin' alright

~Our people been demonssss

Demonized

Demon-ized

Demon eyes

Staring at the skyyyyy

from the Atlantic Ocean

We can't reach up

and I'm convinced that's why

they made heaven so high~

Can we talk for a minute?

Just give me a chance to understand

ain't you the Prince of Darkness? (Then what am I)

ain't you the Prince of Darkness? (Then what am I)

ain't you the Prince of Darkness? (Then what am I)

I'm convinced that the light is poison to our people

we was made in darkness

Show me Satan, show me a friend

in the mirror

lies the past

of your future

your face is

sunken

bones peaking

do you like

what you see?

[Here I Am]

[Heeeree I ammm]

I sing loud to the rain and thunder

Watch meeee

I

Cartwheel in the mud

Get my hands dirty

FILTHY

[Heeeereeee I Ammmm]

Lightning S T R I K E Z

And my hair goes UP

Spikey like a

Pork - u - pine

No, I'm not hospitalized, just

REVITALIZED, just

Mezzzzzmerized

[Here I AM]

I am HERE

I am Here and

There

I am

Here and there, I am

Everywhere!

[Heeereee I ammm]

You better sing it.

Sing for your dead fathers

Sing for your single mothers

Sing for your grandpappy

Sing for your raped grandmama

Sing for your whipped ancestors

Sing for the Black babies at the bottom of the ocean

                              thrown overboard

                cause death was better than chains, I mean

handcuffs

                    I mean shackles, I mean

"Put your hands up! Get on the ground!" I mean

POW, I mean

Ugh! Ain't y'all tired?

I'm crying over here,

I'm trying to sing.

Let me sing

[Hereeee I ammm]

Here I am

Here I am

Let me sing

Let go of me,

I said let go!

[hereee I ammm]

Get off me, man!

[hereee I ammm]

Get off my neck, get off my back

[Here I am here I am]

I can't breathe!

[Here ~ I

Am]

I am weak

My

voice hurts, my

breasts ache, my

back got too many

Too Many

stones

[Here . . . I . . . am]

My kinky hair pullll-ed on

My hoop earrings yanked out bleeeed-ing

My shoes all stepppp-ed on

My face hit and bruiiss-ed

Why are you just watchhhh-ing?

Why are you just watchhhh-ing?

Why are you just watchhh-ing?

We should be singin'

Willful Whispers

Willful whispers float through the halls

They infiltrate my ears

rattle up inside my mind

Whispers of

breaking free

from this existence

No more hopeful shit

I'm tired of all these uplifting poems

Write me something

about the world ending

gunshot wounds

tapeworm parasites

Write me something

realll gooey

The Wanderer

I wander through life

always wondering if it's worth living

The struggle to stay alive

in such a monotone existence

Maybe death

will be invigorating

Your Language

I talk to the letters in the dictionary

The Bs leap and cartwheel

Bitch

Blossom

Bosom

Brass

Brassier

Bug

They say that I am

close to nothingness

All meaning escapes every word

that has ever been said to me

By your mouth

Crazed

Crazy

Cuckoo

I am the naive

Ignorant

Immature

Inexperienced

Ingenuous

Innocent

Perhaps it would be better

if words disappeared

entirely.

Resilience is not my forte

I was told to write a poem on resilience

but all I could do

was let the tears flow out of me

like a city tributary

going from a steady stream

to a bashing, rhythmic pace.

I was told to lift my head up high

but all I could do

was lie in my bed

And count how many intrusive thoughts

invade my conscience.

Resilience is not my forte

Don't call me strong

or a warrior

or powerful

or superwoman

This body of mines

is tired of being all the things

they say a Black woman oughta be

I prefer to stare

into the distance

lose my mind

and never get it back

The Sea Tamer

First published in *Hope Springs Eternal: An Anthology of Hopeful Poetry* (2023) by Simple Simons Press

Inspired by *The Awakening* by Kate Chopin

"Why does she

not float

on the water?"

asks the pointing child.

She stand alone

praying to the horizon

sweep me away

cover me

in sand and pebble

The ocean disobeys

she walks home

Alive

Disappointed,

but alive

Do women not command the sea?

Unshackle the River

First published in *Songs for Wild Ohio* (2023) by Last Exit Press

I wonder how many bodies

are at the bottom of the Ohio

Hands rising up from the water

like burnt twigs

reaching at the Roebling

screaming

FREEDOM

My ancestors—

Those who almost made it

to the promised land

swimmin, boatin, frozen

bodies

screaming

FREEDOM

Blue and Black makes a muddy brown

The Water of Fun

The water of fun

is filled with

shrieks

shrills

sounds

of Black people

swimming

In a white-only pool

Defy God,

dear people

take a bite

out of the tree

of

knowledge

See what fun

lies beyond a world

not meant for you

Occupy it!

Have fun

in the water

Haiku for you

I am in mad love

Come alleviate my soul

Free me from heartbreak

When the Doc told me I was bipolar II

When the Doc told me I was bipolar II,

suddenly everything made sense

No wonder I get lost in my mind

wandering

crying

why the world do us like this?

Us folk

Us folk who inhale stars

and exhale whole universes

Us folk who fly amongst Cardinals—

Our dead ancestors

From behind the veil

No wonder I want to

scream at the top of my lungs

Constantly

Consistently

Insistently

Just all the time

We the folk

We the folk who sing colors

and fiddle to tastes of bitter wine

We the ones

Going out of our minds

Going out of our minds

Going out of our minds

                      Going . . .

Crazy Love

Maybe love isn't meant for me

Perhaps I'm better off

staring at my naked body in the mirror

Make gibberish sounds

and flail my arms above my head

Who will love a quite insane woman like me?

And endure my descent

into madness?

Maybe love isn't meant for me

A nice friend would do

Show Me God

When I put my nose to the inside of a book,

I am reminded of the profound insights of

Toni Morrison, Zora Neale Hurston, June Jordan

The aroma of words revolutionary

taking my imagination to the most radical parts of

heaven

A Poem for Charles

Winner of the Poetry Is Life Publishing "A Father's Heart" poetry contest

First published in *The Voices of Real 8* (2024) by Poetry Is Life Publishing

Charles,

Your daughter wept the day you died

I saw her on grandma's knees

Her shoulders bouncing—

a sing-a-long dot across the screen—

To the rhythm of grief

and pain

Charles,

Your wife cried your name

A Black Woman on the microphone

She sung hymns at your funeral

Let the holy ghost dance

inside her body, limp and loose

She spoke in tongues

Charles,

I heard from my aunts and uncles that

you were a great dad, that

you were the man of the block, that

you took in street kids and taught them

how to count their money, how to

change oil under a car hood

Charles,

The day you called me my mother's name

was the day I discovered

I've got my mother's eyes—her

widow's peak—

A big negroid nose—

Sandy hair from my daddy

Charles,

When you couldn't tell your home

from the grocery store,

those nights you'd wander like a stranger

in a catacomb, already meeting the eyes

of skeletons. Reach your hands out

and death would meet you halfway

Yea, you met your Lord

whom you have so wished

and worshiped and

shouted and

raised your hands towards His heaven

from your home on Earth

Yea, you met your Lord

And I hope He is as wonderful

as you always said He was

I hope one day I can

forgive Him for

taking you

Who was

A father

Who was

My grandfather

I commend your life,

Charles

Ain't Chu Tired?

Ain't chu tired of living

a life dictated by dollar signs?

I know I'm tired.

Ain't chu tired of living

in a country that really don't

give a damn about you?

I know I'm tired.

We supposed to be walking—

strolling—through our lives

like everything's okay

when everything is on fire

Fire! Fire!

I stopped pretending everything was okay

about . . . one . . . two . . .

something years ago

And I'm still tired

exhausted, even.

Palestine on my mind

First published in *For A Better World* (2024) by SOS ART

I've got songs of freedom on my mind

The beat to the rhythm of liberation

drumming in my bones

Even from my condo in Cincinnati

I can hear the screams of the people

They shoutin' "Freedom"

The ground shaking

beneath my feet

of an incoming revolution…

Revolution…

REVOLUTION

White Guilt

your words don't mean nothing if you ain't gone do

nothing

Shake hands with a President

I think I'd fight Andrew Jackson

Kick the shit out of him

Tear up a twenty

Pork Roast

Tearing tough, stringy flesh like it was jerkied

salted meat with a scarlet gravy

teeth chomping, gnawing

Swallowing throats

gulps and

burps

Every cop that has killed one of us

tasty

Blue Lives

We sing the blues

every time a cop spills us red

tomato-faced,

police chase

Blue uniforms come marching in

Aiming for the heart

Love shot

Whose lives are blue?

Da Birdz

There's a cool bird next to my window

He wear sunglasses

To protect his eyes from the sun

He balance on his beak

And fall off sometimes

He stares at me with a

Cool look

Tweet and chirp

Real real cool

He calls his friends over

A flock of da birdz come

Fly flyin'

singin' whistlin'

Bobby McFerrin

They know what to do

They get in formation and dance

And rustle their feathers

And shake their lil tails

And party all mornin' long

They wake up the entire neighborhood

'Fo seven o'clock

'Fo everybody gotta go to work

And whore for green

And be metaphorically whipped

by their 9-5

Da Birdz sing a hip song

to wake you up for wage slavery

every morning

And at night,

when you're exhausted and tired

Spent little time with the kids

Arguing with yo husband

The rent is due,

they quiet

Silent

Mutt Dog

Mutt dog is the baddest dawg in town

He rummages through tasty trash

with his

tail up high and his

ears down low and

he pitter-pats through each brown bin

Find him a bone or two

Spaghetti and meatballs

Like in that Disney movie

Sneak snake into a

hoarder's garage and

steal some rat-poo-infested

canned tuna from the cats

Pounce, you nasty dawg

into the

Dump. His

ribs cracked and

chipped

—from—

The kick

—of—

An angry man

Just come home from work

Lay down on the ground

Play dead

watch a white woman

jogging and

Pick you up

Pat you on the stomach

Roll over, good boy

She'll put you in a

tiny sweater to

show you off to her friends

—a new topic for an essay to write

of how she

saved you

And she'll win some money

off the tribulations

and the hard life

of a mutt dog

'Tis Black or White

Get that

damned gray

outta here

I'm talking about

white ice

Black ice

zebra

candy cane—

mint & licorice

tiger

jaguar

albino

tic tac

white people

white power

white privilege

santa claus

the pope

elvis

condoleezza rice

Black metal

Black comedy

Black person

Black people

Black Powwa

Black Powwa

Black Powwa

I am

Black Radical

white men

white gazes

white world

white mind

thinking

of a white christmas

Black devils

Or Black jesus

GOD

Pick A Side

On Violence

Violence is the voice of the people

When they sing a tune, the world listens as it must

It keeps the wheels turning, violence,

It says, "I want my freedom, and I want it now."

But not all violence is the same, no

The Boss, The Man, The Big Shot

The Capitalist, The Imperialist, The Colonizer

His violence does not have that

same singing tune

It's more like a scream

like a woman getting her clothes torn apart by a

greedy man—

that kind of scream.

For their violence is tying a pregnant woman's

legs together

as she gives birth

And our violence, the

violence of the people,

is the type that frees the mama

And lets her do the slashing.

Molotov Cocktails

Weeeeee throwinnnn'

Weeeeee throwinnnn'

Weeeeee throwinnnn'

Fiery RAGE at our oppressors

Fiery PASSION at our oppressors

Weeeeee throwinnnn'

Everything we've got

We kickin' screamin' schemin' dreamin'

Dreaming of

better days

Remembering Fred

Dear Ancestor Fred,

Fearless Ferocious Fantastic

you are

Tell me, have you radicalized heaven yet?

Are the angels up there wearing black berets

and throwing their fists in the air shouting

"I Am A Revolutionary!"

Have you gathered the dead proletariats

—The dead brothas, the sistahs, and those in between—

and kissed each upon their tired brows?

Say, I remember my 22nd birthday, thinking

I can't believe I outlived you

So young you were but so heavy with

vigor you were

So weighted with

hope you were

I pray that you are

looking down on us and smilin'

that our heads still look to that damned, dreary, polluted

sky

Not So Fairy Tale

I imagine a Golden Palace

where all the beggars go

to get their feet blessed

in oil

A palace where prostitutes

can take off their stilettos

and their fake eyelashes

I suppose the thieves will

put down their itchy, grabbing fingers here

In this palace

lies the promise

of the lumpen

that they will triumph

one day

New Jersey Turnpike

When the oink oink comes struttin' with a gun on his hip

full clip, power trip

trip trippin'

A car full of Black folks

they

no joke, they

lookin' out the back windows

watching the oink oink come walkin'

toward them with a 9mm or ah

AR and

pepper spray

naw, mace

real tangy

on the eyes

blue and black oink oink says

"stick 'em up"

Cowboys and Indians

engine running

negro crying

bean splatter

tightey whitey far right and fighty

oink oink in the pound

he real proud, he

dead on the ground

Let that liquid run cold

run, run, run

in cold blood

hot on they trail

Off the New Jersey Turnpike and

Straight to Cuba

Say "Thank you"

Say "thank you" to the brotha

bumpin' his music on the street

he keepin' the rent down

Saturday Morning Cartoons

I want to thank the Saturday morning cartoons

for keeping me company

While mommy and daddy

fought in the next room.

Ode to the Colored Trumpet Boy

Inspired by "Southwark Fair" (1733) by William Hogarth, oil on canvas

Night sky-painted boy

Pepper-speckled boy

Ash-kissed boy

Toot Toot

your trumpet

amidst the chaos of the scene

Toot Toot

Next to that drummin' white woman

hoot and bap bap bap for the drunk men in the square

Dance, little colored boy, dance

Maybe they'll throw you a coin

Or two

Just when I thought I could write about men

I guess I should apologize for writing this poem

I know nothing about what it means

to be a man

I mean, what is a "man," anyway?

Some kind of sour tropical fruit

found only in the rainforest of Brazil

shaped like a tiny bubble butt?

Or perhaps a man is just a woman without her hands on

her hips

or her nails done

without knowing how to sing lullabies

or not knowing the frustration of a dress with no pockets

A man . . .

That sounds like some type of herb

A tablespoon of it

would be

just enough

Don't look at me like that

You see, Black man, you look at me like I'm a fool

you say,

"Black woman, she ain't got nothing to be scared of"

But I be raped by cops and

my hair yanked as I

get fucked in my ass

You see, Black man, you look me up and down

you say,

"Black woman, she just gotta sit down and be quiet"

But I be loud, I be —LOUD—

I scream on the mountaintop

with my breasts out

and tell God to come at me

My mind is wild

Some would say

Allllll over da place

Dear tree that the white people cut down

I didn't get to say goodbye

Came home from work one day

and saw that you were gone

There was nothing left but a

measly stump.

Wanted to hug you before you left

Tell you how I've graduated from college

got a job now

Adventure of my life

So, goodbye

Sincerely,

An old friend

The Cookout

A fire burns atop the white-speckled coal

Autumn breeze keeps us company

Laughter and

music and

Black folks business

We dance we

play spades

and slam our fists on the table after

a bad play—

four books and a possible

I wish days like this would last forever

Solidarity Party

I hold hands with my Asian brother,

tell him everything's gonna be alright.

Embrace my Native sister,

tell her everything's gonna be alright.

Kiss my Chicano siblings on their cheeks,

tell them everything's gonna be alright.

Sing to my African mother

Cry to my Arab father

Lie next to my Cuban auntie

and wrap myself in the arms of my Haitian uncle.

The Cookout Part Two

Hand-picked collard greens

in a pot with

smoked turkey

basted in butter

Five cheese macaroni

a dash of milk

paprika and

salt to taste

Four potatoes mashed

and topped with

thickened gravy

A golden honey ham

sliced

surrounded by foliage

Peach cobbler

with a braided sugar crust

and upside-down cake

with pineapple chunks

Need I go on?

Bee Booty

A big ole bee

landed its all black and yellow self

right on my lap

I think it wanted to whisper

something about

dead flowers in the garden

It looked up at me

and said

"them azaleas dead again"

Dead?

Dead like Tupac?

Dead like Rock N Roll?

That bee said

"Yep,

Like a good poet."

So, I gets on the ground

And pray to Jesus

                    Resurrect the flowers

Let this bee booty

Do its duty

Yessuh

the bee prepare his stinger

Poking out his behind

He stab stab stab

Then sprouts a daisy

Rejoice

Rejoice with your mothers and your fathers

Rejoice with grandma and grandpappy

Yell out your bedroom window

say "Lord, We Free"

Tell the clouds move out the way

Let some sun in

Let some light in

Let God in

Hold hands with your Black folk

Ring shout

We Free

Free

Free

Free

Free...

Got my eye on it

I've got my eye on it

I can smell it

feel it

I can

taste it on the tip of my tongue

I can see down the way

Clouds spreading to reveal the view

Rain letting up, and

winds calming

Almost got it

in my reach

That liberation

It's in my hands now

www.ingramcontent.com/pod-product-compliance
Lightning Source LLC
Chambersburg PA
CBHW020338010526
44119CB00035B/443/J